EGG TO CHICKEN

LIFE CYCLES

Words that look like **this** can be found in the glossary on page 24.

London Borough of Havering	
90120000032563	
Askews & Holts	South Hx
J571.818	£12.99
10/5/17	

©2017
Book Life
King's Lynn
Norfolk PE30 4LS

ISBN: 978-1-78637-145-4

All rights reserved
Printed in Malaysia

Written by:
Grace Jones
Edited by:
Charlie Ogden
Designed by:
Danielle Rippengill

A catalogue record for this book is available from the British Library.

EGG TO CHICKEN

Page 4	What Is a Life Cycle?
Page 5	What Is a Chicken?
Page 6	Eggs
Page 8	Growing Eggs
Page 10	Hatching Chicks
Page 12	Growing Chicks
Page 14	Chickens
Page 16	Food
Page 18	Clucking Chickens
Page 20	World Record Breakers
Page 22	Life Cycle of a Chicken
Page 23	Get Exploring!
Page 24	Glossary and Index

WHAT IS A LIFE CYCLE?

All animals and humans go through different stages in their life as they grow. This is called a life cycle.

Baby → Child → Adult

WHAT IS A CHICKEN?

A chicken is a bird. Chickens have two legs, two wings, a beak and they are covered in feathers.

EGGS

A female chicken, called a hen, makes a nest on the ground to lay her eggs in. The nest is mostly made of straw.

Nest

Eggs

Hens usually lay around one egg a day.

A hen lays her eggs inside a nest. Inside each egg is a tiny dot, called an embryo, that will eventually grow into a chicken.

GROWING EGGS

A hen sits on her eggs to keep them warm. This is called brooding. This is an important job that helps the eggs to grow.

A group of eggs is called a clutch.

Inside the egg, the tiny chicken embryo is growing. It eats the yellow yolk inside the egg for its food. The hard shell of the egg protects the embryo.

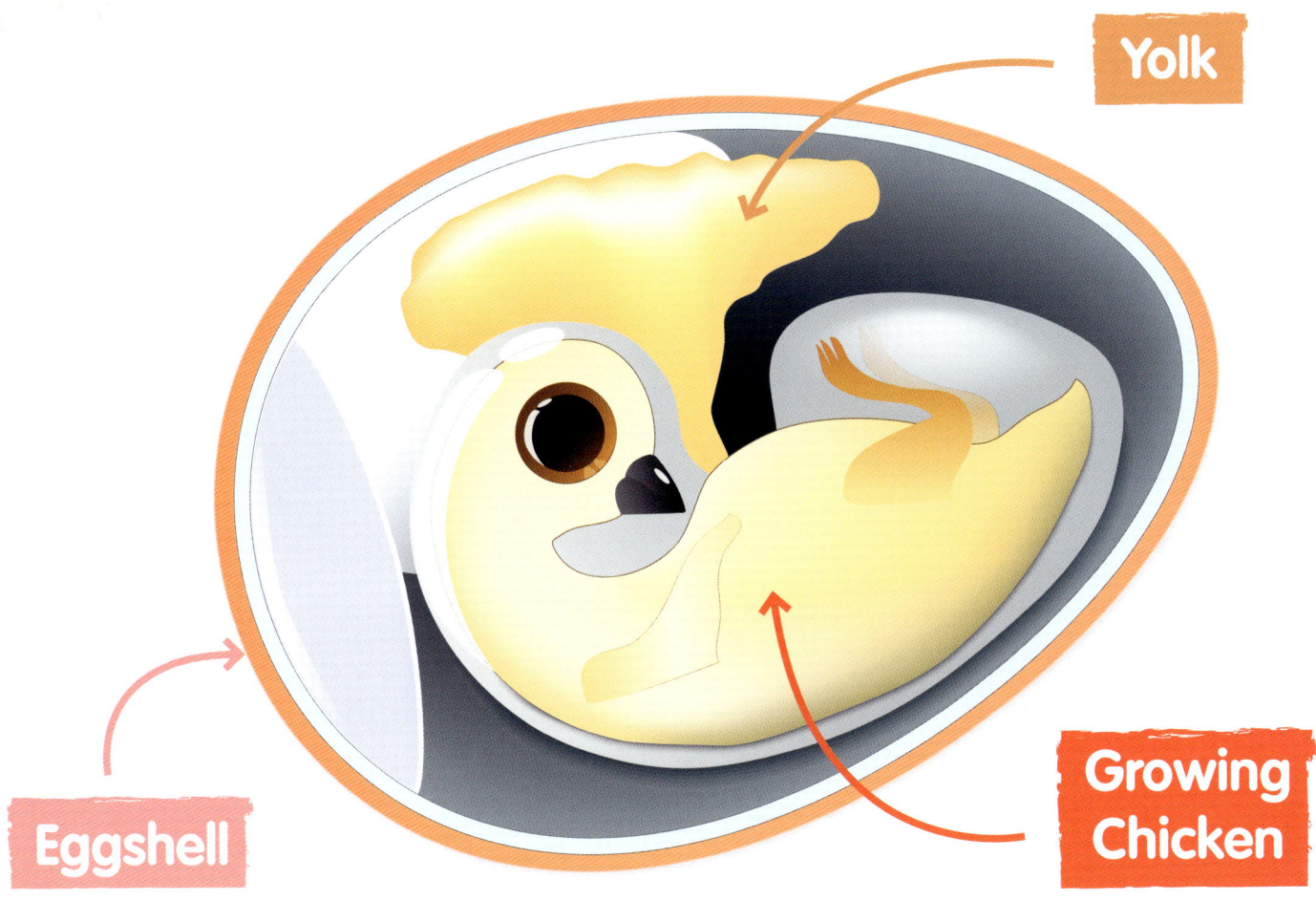

Yolk

Eggshell

Growing Chicken

HATCHING CHICKS

This chick is breaking out of its egg.

This is a newly-hatched chick.

After around three weeks of growing, the baby chicken breaks out of its egg. This is called hatching. The baby chicken that comes out is called a chick.

The hen keeps her chicks warm under her wings. After another two weeks, the chicks will be strong enough to explore outside the nest.

Chicks have very fluffy feathers just after they have hatched.

GROWING CHICKS

Chicks make a cheeping noise so that their mother can find them.

Chicks look for their own food. If they are outside, chicks will look for worms and bugs on the ground.

As they grow bigger, the chicks will lose their fluffy feathers and grow bigger, stronger feathers. They will also grow **combs** on their heads.

Feathers

Comb

Chickens' combs are usually red.

CHICKENS

It takes between six and eight months for chicks to grow into adult chickens. After this, the young hens are ready to lay eggs of their own.

Pullet

A hen that is under a year old is called a pullet.

Male chickens are called roosters or cockerels. They are usually larger than hens. They also have larger combs and longer tail feathers.

Comb

Tail Feathers

This is a bantam rooster.

FOOD

Grain

This chicken is eating grain.

Nearly all chickens are **domesticated**, which means that they do not live in the wild. Instead, they live on farms or are kept as pets. Chickens are fed by the people who own them.

If chickens spend their time outside, they will look for food to eat on the ground. They often eat the bugs and seeds they find in the **soil**.

These chickens are looking for food on the ground.

CLUCKING CHICKENS

There are over 65 different types of chicken and one of the strangest is the Silkie. These chickens have fluffy white feathers, black skin and blue **earlobes**.

Silkie Chicken

Chickens make lots of sounds to tell each other different things. Mother hens can tell their chicks when they have found food.

WORLD RECORD BREAKERS

The Most Eggs Laid

The most eggs laid in one year is 371. They were laid by a type of chicken called a white leghorn.

The Heaviest Chicken Egg
Weight: 454 grams

Fun Fact: That's about the same weight as a football!

LIFE CYCLE OF A CHICKEN

Get Exploring!

Ask a parent or guardian whether you can visit a farm near to where you live. What animals can you see? Can you spot any chickens?

GLOSSARY

combs soft body parts found on chickens' heads
domesticated kept as a pet or raised on a farm
earlobes the soft skin near the bottom of ears
soil the upper layer of earth where plants grow

INDEX

brooding 8
chicks 10–14, 19, 22
cockerels 15
eggs 6–10, 14, 20–22
feathers 5, 11, 13, 15, 18
food 9, 12, 16–17, 19

hatching 10–12, 22
hens 6–8, 11, 14–15, 19, 22
nests 6–7, 11, 22
Silkie chickens 18

PHOTO CREDITS

Photocredits: Abbreviations: l-left, r-right, b-bottom, t-top, c-centre, m-middle. All images are courtesy of Shutterstock.com. Front Cover — Tsekhmister. 1 – Tsekhmister. 2 – Eric Isselee. 3t – Coprid. 3m – Iurii Kachkovskyi. 3b – Szasz-Fabian Jozsef. 4l – Oksana Kuzmina. 4m – studioloco. 4r – Ljupco Smokovski. 5 – stockphoto mania. 6 – Gavran333. 7 – Kiss Gabor Balazs. 8 – Chokniti Khongchum. 9 – Designua. 10l – Rarin Lee. 10r – Anneka. 11 – Andia. 12 – Alex Ionas. 13 – Szasz-Fabian Jozsef. 14 – Menna. 15 – ananaline. 16 – Borja Andreu. 17 – FiledIMAGE. 18 – Eric Isselee. 19 – Ivonne Wierink. 20 – MarijaPiliponyte. 21 – Coprid. 22t – Kiss Gabor Balazs. 22l – Menna. 22r – Andia. 23 – Subbotina Anna, Images are courtesy of Shutterstock.com. With thanks to Getty Images, Thinkstock Photo and iStockphoto.